something beginning with me...

as I go to secondary school

First published in Great Britain in 2012 by
Something beginning with me Ltd

Copyright, 2012 Erica Hurley
Published April 2012
ISBN: boy - 978-0-9567112-2-9
       girl - 978-0-9567112-3-6

Dedicated to Joseph & Lewis Donovan

The moral right of the authors and referees has been asserted

All rights reserved

No part of this workbook may be used or reproduced in any form or by any means electronic or mechanical without the written permission of the publisher or the author.

Publisher: Something beginning with me Ltd
Web address: www.sbwm.co
E-mail: erica@sbwm.co

Cover design: So design consultants Ltd.
www.so-design.co.uk

Models in cover design: Tom Astley
www.tomastley.com

Something beginning with me...

How to use this book:

This book is for you to use like a diary, it will help you to record where you are as you start to make changes in your life as you move up to secondary school.

Looking at where you are starting from and where you would like to be, it is a place for you to write down your dreams, goals and ideas, to help you understand more about what's important to you.

Answer the questions in each chapter to find out the things that you enjoy and the things that annoy you, the things that you'd like to carry on doing and the things you'd like to stop doing; and then use chapter 6 to set yourself some goals to help you to get what you want...

We all have things about ourselves that we like, and other things that we would change if we could. Some of these things we cannot change, but for those that we can, we may need a little help and support to make sure we can achieve them.

This book is set out so there are parts that will help you look at how you feel about yourself and others and help you to set some goals around these if you want to. Most importantly there is plenty of space, so that you can check when you reach these goals and think about setting yourself some new ones!

We are all different, some of us like writing things down, others prefer to draw pictures and others may just use this book as a kind of scrap-book. All of these are fine! This is your book, so fill it in however you like, as long as you do it in a way that means something to you.

Index

Chapter 1 - Who I am... page 7-23

Chapter 2 - Where you'll find me... page 25-49

Chapter 3 - Things I do... page 51-77

Chapter 4 - Who I know... page 79-03

Chapter 5 - More about me... page 95-111

Chapter 6 - My goals, dreams and targets... page 113-145

Useful stuff...page 147-159
- Pie chart - 148-149
- Mind map - 150-151
- Star signs - 152
- Chinese years - 153
- Countries of the world - 154-157

Something beginning with me...

Chapter 1:
'Who I am...'

About me...

Name: Kelisha ann sheppard

Today's date:

Where I got this book: from hanham high

My friends call me: Kelisha, K, Kellogs

Date of birth:

Star sign*: caprocorn

Born in the Chinese year* of: Sheep

* see usefule stuff on pages 152-153

Nationality:

Religion:

Favourite colour: Blue

My best friend: ~~nobody~~ lacie ♡

My other friends: Maryam, Lacie?, Nadine

My heroes/heroines: ~~freddie hollyoaks~~ /Ashley/ charlie chaplin. cameron diaz.

If I wasn't me I'd like to be... ~~Beyonce~~ cameron diaz

Height:

Weight:

My other measurements/clothes sizes:

Favourite jokes/quotes/sayings:

The thing I like most about myself is: I'm glad about who I am.

If there was one thing I could change about myself it would be: To have Much more freinds.

What I look like:

My hair colour, length and style, eye colour, clothes I wear everyday, clothes I would choose to wear for special occasions, or when I'm relaxing. My favourite clothes, shoes, jeans, jewellery, bags, trainers, sports kit etc...

I would describe myself as...

My family:

My mother, father, step-mother, step-father, carer, foster-parents, brothers and sisters, half-brothers and sisters, grandparents, great-grand parents, aunties, uncles and cousins who are important to me...

My family:

Who I am like from the people I have listed and who I am not like and why...

I am like:

Because:

I am not like:

Because:

Recent photographs of me and my family:

Recent photographs of me and my family:

Recent photographs of me and my family:

Recent photographs of me and my family:

My most recent birthday - I was __11yrs__ years old:

How I celebrated my birthday and who I did this with.

The presents I received and who from:

bike, clothes, timberlends, sweets, DVD's lots more

Pictures and other reminders of my __10__ th birthday:

Pictures and other reminders of my __11__th birthday:

Pictures and other reminders of my __12__th birthday:

"Life is ten percent fact and ninety percent attitude"

Something beginning with me...

Chapter 2:
'Where you'll find me...'

Where you'll find me:...

Where I spend my time, places I visit, places I stay and places I travel to...

Where I live:

1 nublets hill
st george
bristol
BS5 8BH

I have lived here since:

2014

Where else I live from time to time:

Lots of diffrent places

A bit about my home:

The kind of home we live in, the size, how close we are to our neighbours (terraced, house, apartment, detached etc), the number of rooms, bedrooms, bathrooms, garden etc.

Who lives here with me, family and pets and if I share a room with anyone.

Paula
Kiera
amy
George
Kesha
Ebny
Mummy
Daddy
a'shaneya
Madison
cody
much more.

Other close family who don't live here with me:

My mum, dad, 2 sissters, two bros.

Where they live and how far away this is: ~~Hribilits~~
1 nevison place Lockleaze.

How often I get to see them: ~~Once evrey~~
Once evrey 6 weeks.

The area we live in:

People live in lots of different kinds of places, some in the countryside, others in the city, in small or large towns. The people who live in these kinds of areas are all very different. Here's something about my local area, its size and surrounding area and the kind of people who live here.

Where I lived before:

What it was like, how long we lived there. if it was better or worse than where we live now and why:

Where I'm going to secondary school:

Name of my school: Fulton avenue Junior school / F.A.J.S

Address:

I've been going to this school since: nursrey.

Uniform at new secondary school: black Jumper with Bage of Mouse course.

Uniform at previous primary school:

Where I went to primary school: F.A.J.S

What I liked about my primary school: MY freinds.

How I used to get to and from primary school: tAXi.

How I'll get to and from secondary school: WALK

About my new secondary school:

The kind of school it is, the size, how many children, how many teachers, how many classes, how many children in my class, sports we play, other activities:

What I like about my new school:

I made new freind's

What I don't like about my new school:

teachers

How it's different to my previous school:

My Class name is: 8y3

My Class tutor is: choa miss david

The School Head is: mr beavean

My new friends in this school are:
bethan,
georgiea
callum G
Harvey P
porchea
Jake Crain

My favourite teachers are:
miss P

Subjects I am studying:	Teacher	Grade at last exam

Subjects I am studying:	Teacher	Grade at last exam

My favourite subjects at my previous school were:

history
science
PE
maths

My favourite subjects at my new secondary school are:

History
PE
science
cooking

Subjects I would like to study further are:

cooking pt.

Subjects I would like to stop if I am able:

Virtual places you'll find me:

My favourite on-line networks, friends and games, how much time I spend on these and who I meet or talk to there...

	Use this (yes/no)	Who I talk to this way:
e-mail	No	Nobody
mobile phone	Yes	freinds
text (phone)	Yes	freinds
skype	No	No
facebook	No	No
msn/ windows live	No	No
twitter	No	No
myspace	No	No
bbm	No	No
nintendo	No	No
google+	No	No
playstation	No	No
steam	No	No
other...	No	No

Where else you will find me:

Family and friends' homes, outdoor places, parks, fields, clubs, open spaces, cinemas, church, shops, school, fast-food joints etc.:

How I get around between these places:

Who I rely on to get me there, and what kinds of transport we use.:

Where I am allowed to walk or ride on my own or with my friends:

Where I spend my time:

This is a pie chart* of how much time I spend at each of these places per week.

Each slice is about 10.5 hours of time...

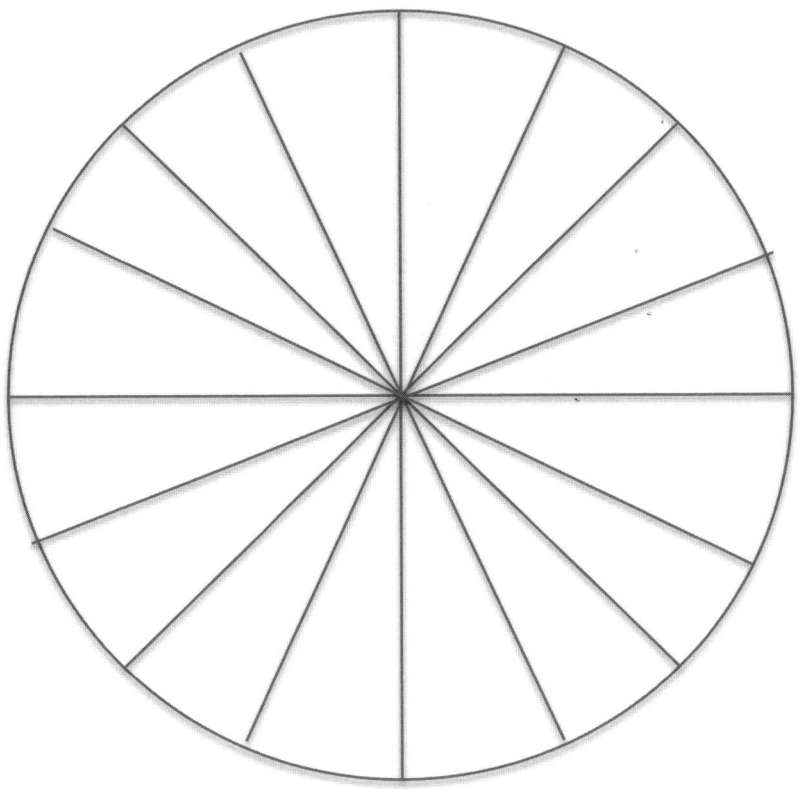

*see pages 148-149

This is how much time I would like to spend at each of these places per week...

Each slice is about 10.5 hours of time...

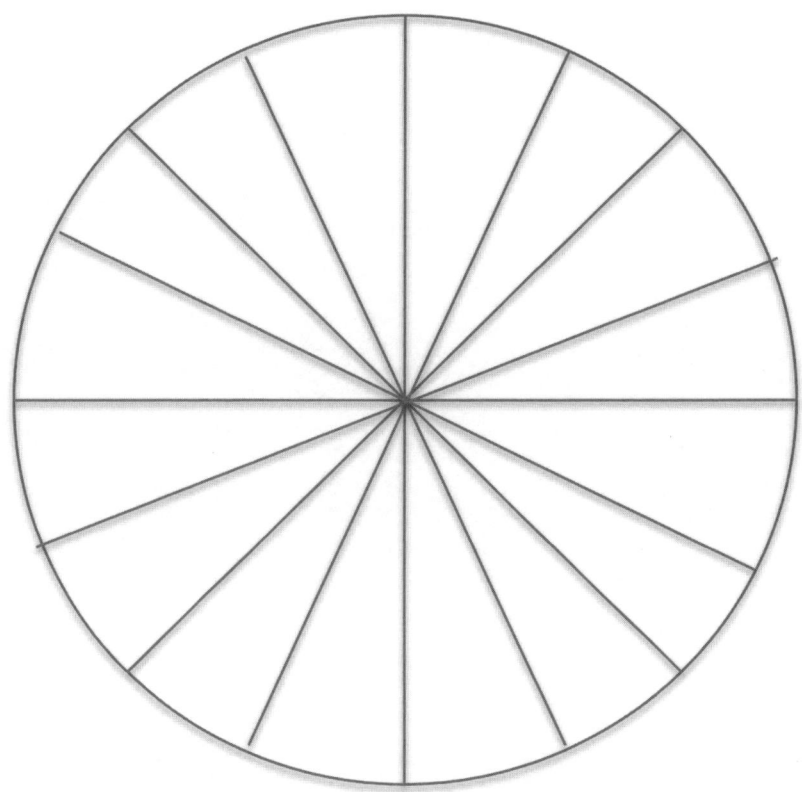

Go to pages 130-131 to set yourself some goals to achieve this

School holidays:

What I did during the holidays this year and who I did this with. Where we went and how we got there, how long we stayed for, the things I did and if I'd like to do these again sometime:

Photographs and other reminders of my most recent holiday time:

Photographs and other reminders of my most recent holiday time:

Photographs and other reminders of my most recent holiday time:

Places I have been...

dawlish warrens

*see pages 154-157 for a list of countries of the world

Places I would like to go one day...

Jamaea

Use the questions in chapter 6 to set yourself some goals or targets in this area

"The future belongs to those who believe in the beauty of their dreams"

Eleanor Roosevelt

Something beginning with me...

Chapter 3:
'Things I do...'

The things you'll see me doing...

We all like to do different things, sometimes on our own and sometimes with other people, This section explores some of the things I like to do and those I don't.

If I have time to myself, I like to...

I'm very good at...

I'm not so good at...

Playing/relaxing:

Things I like to do when I am not at school - my favourite sports, games, hobbies, interests, web sites, sports teams, etc:

Things that I don't like having to do and what I do to avoid these if possible:

Use teh questions in chapter 6 to set yourself some goals or targets in this area

Listening to things:

My favourite music, songs, radio shows, favourite bands, groups, orchestras, musicians etc:

Things I don't like having to listen to and the reasons why:

My top 10 favourite songs/tracks:

	Name of song	Artist/band
1	Silento	wip
2	black magic	little mix
3	wont to want me	Jason derulo
4	drag me down	one direction
5		
6		
7		
8		
9		
10		

When I was younger, my favourite top 10 songs used to be:

(you may want to ask someone to help with this bit)

	Track or song	If I still like this or not & why
1		
2		
3		
4		
5		
6		
7		
8		
9		
10		

Watching:

Things I like to watch - tv programmes, films, sports activities, youtube, comedy, theatre:

People I like to watch - my favourite people, groups, celebrities, sports people, football teams etc...:

Things I don't like having to watch and why:

Top 10 TV programmes:

	Title	Why I like it...
1	hollyoaks	because i use to watch it with mum
2	eastenders	because i use to watch it with my mum and it's fun
3	coronation street	it's good
4		
5		
6		
7		
8		
9		
10		

When I was younger, my top 10 TV programmes used to be:

	Title	If I still like it or not & why...
1		
2		
3		
4		
5		
6		
7		
8		
9		
10		

How has this changed?

Do you think it will change again as you get older?

My top 10 films of all time:

	Title	Why I like it/best bits...
1		
2		
3		
4		
5		

	Title	Why I like it/best bits...
6		
7		
8		
9		
10		

Reading:

We all have to read things at different times, sometimes it's for school or for our chosen hobbies and other reading is just for fun. These are the things that I like to read and why, including my favourite books, comics, magazines, newspapers etc:

Things I like to read:

Things I don't like having to read and why:

My favourite books, authors & characters:

	Book/author/character	Why
1		
2		
3		
4		
5		

	Book/author/character	Why
6		
7		
8		
9		
10		

Eating and drinking:

My favourite foods, snacks, treats, restaurants, take-aways etc:

Things I don't like to eat or drink and why:

Foods and drinks I've never tried but would like to try one day:

Things I like to cook, make or prepare and my favourite recipes/chefs/cooks:

"Talk to old people -
they know cool stuff you
don't..."

Something beginning with me...

Chapter 4:
'Who I know...'

Who you'll see me with...

These are the people I see and talk with most often. Some of them I like more than others, some make me laugh and make me happy, others annoy and frustrate me! Here are their names and what I think about each of them, this list includes my family, friends, teachers, and others...

Use the questions in chapter 6 at the back of the book to set yourself some goals/targets in this area

Who/ relationship	What I think about them/how they make me feel...

Who/ relationship	What I think about them/how they make me feel...

Who/ relationship	What I think about them/how they make me feel…

Who/ relationship	What I think about them/how they make me feel...

Who you'll see me with...

This is a mind map* of the people I spend my time with.

Who you'll see me with...

This is a mind map* of the people I spend my time with.

* see pages 150-151

Using the map that I've drawn, these are the people that I'd like to spend more time with, to talk with more or to get closer to and some ideas about how I can to do this...

Name	What I'm going to do...	When...

Name	What I'm going to do...	When...

Who I miss:

As we grow up there are people who move away and we lose contact with, or people and pets who die and we can no longer see them. This is especially true when we change schools. These are some of the people or pets who I no longer see and why I miss them...

These are some of the things I can do to remember them when I need to:

This is how I can contact them if I need to:

Who I go to for help:

As we grow there are certain people who help us in lots of different ways, This may be with advice, ideas or comfort. They may cheer us up, make us laugh, listen to our problems, share our concern or celebrate our successes.

These are the people I go to for help and what I go to them for:

If I want to find out something I will ask/go to:

Where I go to make new friends/contacts:

There are lots of places we can go to find new friends and people who share our interests and hobbies or to meet with our existing friends. These are the ways I do this:

Where I go to make new friends/contacts:

Use the questions in chapter 6 to set yourself some goals or targets in this area

"If you believe you can or believe you can't you're probably right"

Something beginning with me...

Chapter 5:
'More about me...'

Things I'm good at:

These are some of the things I am good at or that I know about, There are lots of things that I do well and there are also things that I have to work at, but really enjoy doing anyway:

These are some of the things that I am learning to do and how I'm getting on with them, including goals that I've set myself in improving these new skills, talents or abilities:

Things I'm not good at:

These are the things I don't like doing, or will avoid having to do if possible:

Use the questions in chapter 6 to set yourself some goals or targets in this area

My 'best day ever':

If I could plan my best day ever, this is who would be there, what I'd be doing, what the other people would be doing, what I'd find fun, interesting relaxing, etc. and why:

My 'worst day ever':

If I had to think of my worst day ever, this is who would be there, what we'd be doing, what I'd find boring, annoying, frustrating etc. and why:

Things that are important to me:

These are some of my favourite things, games, toys, jewellery, photos, pets, reminders etc.

Why they are important to me or what they remind me of:

Thing...	Why...

Thing...	Why...

Things that I believe:

I should...

I ought to...

I must remember to...

It would be good if other people...

It's really important that we...

It's not nice to...

The world would be a better place if...

If only I could...

Then...

When I am older it will be important for me to...

When I am older it will mean that I am allowed to...

When I have to sit my secondary school exams it will mean that I will have to...

My friends are important to me because...

My family is important to me because...

It's important for me to be able to...

It's important that I am allowed to...

It's important for me to have...

If only others would...

Then...

Things that are important to me:

We all value different things in life, when we value something and it is important to us, then we will try to do things that make sure that we get more of these. There are also things which are not important to us and we don't care if we have them or not. These are the 5 things most important for me (choose your top 5 and mark these with a line, cirle or a highlighter pen)

Values:

acceptance • activity • admiration • approval • attention • authority • beauty • caring • challenge • cleanliness • collaboration • communication • competition • co-operation • courage • creativity • dignity • difference • education • efficiency • entertainment • equality • excellence • excitement • expression • fairness • faith • fame • family • freedom • friends • fulfilment • fun • grace • happiness • harmony • health • helping • honesty • image • independence • integrity • insight • innovation • joy • justice • knowledge • learning • logic • looks • love • manners • obedience • order • others • pain avoidance • partnership • peace • perseverance • popularity • power • quiet • reality • reason • recognition • revolution • rewards • respect • relationships • responsibility • religion •

safety · security · self-reliance ·
self-sacrifice · serenity · sharing · silence ·
simplicity · space · style · spirited ·
status · success · time · tolerance · truth ·
trust · uniqueness · variety · vitality ·
wealth · winning · wisdom · zest ·

Top 5 things that are important to me:
1
2
3
4
5

Things I've done that I'm proud of:

Recently:

This year:

As far back as I can remember:

Things that I'm not proud of:

Recently:

This year:

As far back as I can remember:

I feel most confident when...

The people who help me feel most confident are:

I lack confidence when...

The people who make me feel less confident are:

Use the questions in chapter 6 to set yourself some goals or targets in this area

"When you change what you believe, you can change what you can do"

Something beginning with me...

Chapter 6:
'My goals, dreams and targets...'

The questions on the following pages will help you to think more about your goals, dreams and targets so that you can do something about them and give yourself the best chance of achieving them.

Take your time to think about how you answer these questions...

What I want to be/what I want to do when I leave secondary school:

	My dreams/goals/targets	How and where I want to do this
1		
2		
3		

Use pages 116-121 to work through each of these goals

Goal/dream/target number: 1 - when I leave secondary school

My goal/dream/target written in **positive** words (what I want to have, not what I don't want to have!!)

I want to achieve this by...

I want to be able to do this when I am...

When I have achieved this other people will see me...

They will hear me...

I will feel...

To achieve this I will have to...

When I achieve this, I may have to stop...

Because...

To achieve this I will need to learn how to...

I will need help from...

They will need to help me to...

When I achieve this, my next goal will be to...

Today I will make a start on this goal, by taking this one small step - I will...

Goal/dream/target number: 2 - when I leave secondary school

My goal/dream/target written in **positive** words (what I want to have, not what I don't want to have!!)

I want to achieve this by...

I want to be able to do this when I am...

When I have achieved this other people will see me...

They will hear me...

I will feel...

To achieve this I will have to...

When I achieve this, I may have to stop...

Because...

To achieve this I will need to learn how to...

I will need help from...

They will need to help me to...

When I achieve this, my next goal will be to...

Today I will make a start on this goal, by taking this one small step - I will...

Goal/dream/target number: 3 - when I leave secondary school

My goal/dream/target written in **positive** words (what I want to have, not what I don't want to have!!)

I want to achieve this by...

I want to be able to do this when I am...

When I have achieved this other people will see me...

They will hear me...

I will feel...

To achieve this I will have to...

When I achieve this, I may have to stop...

Because...

To achieve this I will need to learn how to...

I will need help from...

They will need to help me to...

When I achieve this, my next goal will be to...

Today I will make a start on this goal, by taking this one small step - I will...

What I want to be/able to do when I am 14:

	My dreams/goals/targets	How and where I want to do this
1		
2		
3		

Use pages 124-129 to work through each of these goals

Goal/dream/target number: 1 - when I am 14

My goal/dream/target written in **positive** words (what I want to have, not what I don't want to have!!)

I want to achieve this by...

I want to be able to do this when I am...

When I have achieved this other people will see me...

They will hear me...

I will feel...

To achieve this I will have to...

When I achieve this, I may have to stop...

Because...

To achieve this I will need to learn how to...

I will need help from...

They will need to help me to...

When I achieve this, my next goal will be to...

Today I will make a start on this goal, by taking this one small step - I will...

Goal/dream/target number: 2 - when I am 14

My goal/dream/target written in **positive** words (what I want to have, not what I don't want to have!!)

I want to achieve this by...

I want to be able to do this when I am...

When I have achieved this other people will see me...

They will hear me...

I will feel...

To achieve this I will have to...

When I achieve this, I may have to stop...

Because...

To achieve this I will need to learn how to...

I will need help from...

They will need to help me to...

When I achieve this, my next goal will be to...

Today I will make a start on this goal, by taking this one small step - I will...

Goal/dream/target number: 3 - when I am 14

My goal/dream/target written in **positive** words (what I want to have, not what I don't want to have!!)

I want to achieve this by...

I want to be able to do this when I am...

When I have achieved this other people will see me...

They will hear me...

I will feel...

To achieve this I will have to...

When I achieve this, I may have to stop...

Because...

To achieve this I will need to learn how to...

I will need help from...

They will need to help me to...

When I achieve this, my next goal will be to...

Today I will make a start on this goal, by taking this one small step - I will...

What I want to be/what I want to do for me right now:

	My dreams/goals/targets	How and where I want to do this
1		
2		
3		

What I want to be/what I want to do for me right now:

	My dreams/goals/targets	How and where I want to do this
4		
5		
6		

Use pages 131-143 to work through each of these goals, go back through the book for ideas on goals to set yourself for now

Goal/dream/target number: 1 - for me right now

My goal/dream/target written in **positive** words (what I want to have, not what I don't want to have!!)

I want to achieve this by...

I want to be able to do this when I am...

When I have achieved this other people will see me...

They will hear me...

I will feel...

To achieve this I will have to...

When I achieve this, I may have to stop...

Because...

To achieve this I will need to learn how to...

I will need help from...

They will need to help me to...

When I achieve this, my next goal will be to...

Today I will make a start on this goal, by taking this one small step - I will...

Goal/dream/target number: 2 - for me right now

My goal/dream/target written in **positive** words (what I want to have, not what I don't want to have!!)

I want to achieve this by...

I want to be able to do this when I am...

When I have achieved this other people will see me...

They will hear me...

I will feel...

To achieve this I will have to...

When I achieve this, I may have to stop...

Because...

To achieve this I will need to learn how to...

I will need help from...

They will need to help me to...

When I achieve this, my next goal will be to...

Today I will make a start on this goal, by taking this one small step - I will...

Goal/dream/target number: 3 - for me right now

My goal/dream/target written in **positive** words (what I want to have, not what I don't want to have!!)

I want to achieve this by...

I want to be able to do this when I am...

When I have achieved this other people will see me...

They will hear me...

I will feel...

To achieve this I will have to...

When I achieve this, I may have to stop...

Because...

To achieve this I will need to learn how to...

I will need help from...

They will need to help me to...

When I achieve this, my next goal will be to...

Today I will make a start on this goal, by taking this one small step - I will...

Goal/dream/target number: 4 - for me right now

My goal/dream/target written in **positive** words (what I want to have, not what I don't want to have!!)

I want to achieve this by...

I want to be able to do this when I am...

When I have achieved this other people will see me...

They will hear me...

I will feel...

To achieve this I will have to...

When I achieve this, I may have to stop...

Because...

To achieve this I will need to learn how to...

I will need help from...

They will need to help me to...

When I achieve this, my next goal will be to...

Today I will make a start on this goal, by taking this one small step - I will...

Goal/dream/target number: 5 - for me right now

My goal/dream/target written in **positive** words (what I want to have, not what I don't want to have!!)

I want to achieve this by...

I want to be able to do this when I am...

When I have achieved this other people will see me...

They will hear me...

I will feel...

To achieve this I will have to...

When I achieve this, I may have to stop...

Because...

To achieve this I will need to learn how to...

I will need help from...

They will need to help me to...

When I achieve this, my next goal will be to...

Today I will make a start on this goal, by taking this one small step - I will...

Goal/dream/target number: 6 - for me right now

My goal/dream/target written in **positive** words (what I want to have, not what I don't want to have!!)

I want to achieve this by...

I want to be able to do this when I am...

When I have achieved this other people will see me...

They will hear me...

I will feel...

To achieve this I will have to...

When I achieve this, I may have to stop...

Because...

To achieve this I will need to learn how to...

I will need help from...

They will need to help me to...

When I achieve this, my next goal will be to...

Today I will make a start on this goal by, taking this one small step - I will...

When I have achieved all of my dreams, goals and targets...

It will be...

I will feel...

You will see me...

It will show...

Others will say...

My next steps will be to...

Something beginning with me...

'Useful stuff...'

How to do a pie chart (or circle graph)

On pages 42-43 you can do a pie chart of where you spend your time, this is a simple way of showing how much of your time you spend on differnt things.

If you imagine the whole pie is 100% of your time and there are 168 hours in a week, if you spend half of your time on one activity and the other half on another, then you would draw a line down the middle of the pie to show 50% on each side (84 hours).

It's more likely that you spend your time on lots of different things and you can estimate how big a slice to allow using these guidelines.

hours	segments of pie
63 hours	6
52.5 hours	5
42 hours	4
31.5 hours	3
21 hours	2
10.5 hours	1
5 hours	0.5

Example pie chart:

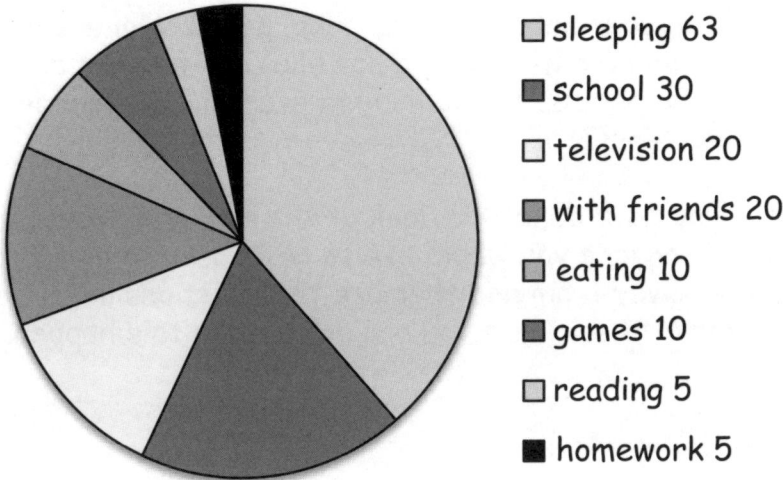

How to draw a mind map:

On page 84-85 you will draw a mind map of people you have listed on pages 80-83.

Put your own name in a bubble at the centre of the map and then add in the people in the list by adding each of their names in a bubble.

The closer they are to you, the closer you put their bubble to your bubble on your map, people who are not close to you (or who you do not like) put further away from your bubble. try to include everyone on your list on pages 80-83.

Once you have done this, look at the map and decide if there is anyone you would like to get closer to or move further away from and then use the questions in chapter 6 to say what you can do to make this happen.

Your completed map should look something like this...

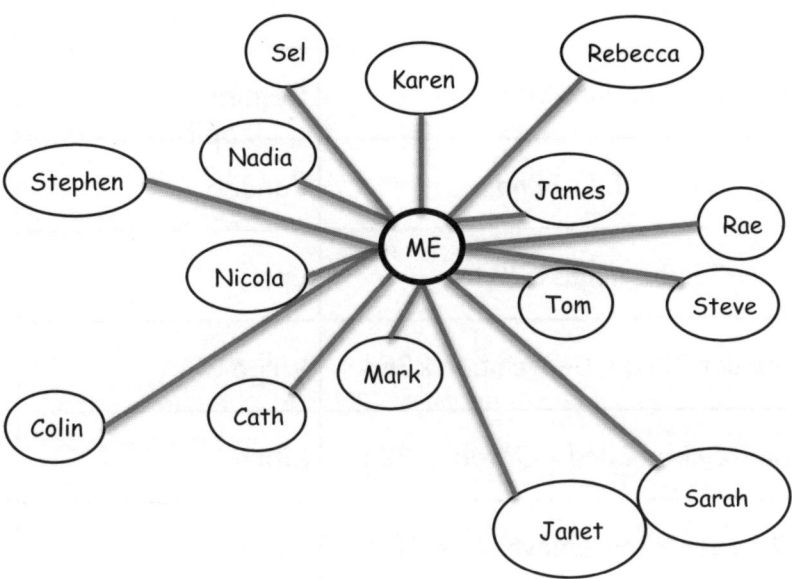

Star signs:

Birthday	Your star sign
March 21st - April 19th	Aries
April 20th - May 20th	Taurus
May 21st - June 20th	Gemini
June 21st - July 22nd	Cancer
July 23rd - August 22nd	Leo
August 23rd - September 22nd	Virgo
September 23rd - October 22nd	Libra
October 23rd - November 21st	Scorpio
November 22nd - December 21st	Sagittarius
December 22nd - January 19th	Capricorn
January 20th - February 18th	Aquarius
February 19th - March 20th	Pisces

Chinese years

The Chinese Lunar calendar names each of the twelve years after an animal. Legend has it that the Lord Buddha summoned all the animals to come to him before he departed from earth.
Only twelve came to bid him farewell and as a reward he named a year after each one in the order they arrived. The Chinese believe the animal ruling the year in which a person is born is the animal that hides in your heart.

Rat	1948	1960	1972	1984	1996	2008
Ox	1949	1961	1973	1985	1997	2009
Tiger	1950	1962	1974	1986	1998	2010
Rabbit	1951	1963	1975	1987	1999	2011
Dragon	1952	1964	1976	1988	2000	2012
Snake	1953	1965	1977	1989	2001	2013
Horse	1954	1966	1978	1990	2002	2014
Sheep	1955	1967	1979	1991	2003	2015
Monkey	1956	1968	1980	1992	2004	2016
Rooster	1957	1969	1981	1993	2005	2017
Dog	1958	1970	1982	1994	2006	2018
Boar	1959	1971	1983	1995	2007	2019

Countries of the world...

Afghanistan	Brazil	Denmark
Akrotiri	Brunei	Dhekelia
Albania	Bulgaria	Djibouti
Algeria	Burkina Faso	Dominica
Andorra	Burma	Dom Replublic
Angola	Burundi	Ecaudor
Anguilla	Cambodia	Egypt
Antartica	Cameroon	El Salvador
Antigua	Canada	England
Argentina	Cape Verde	Equatorial G'nea
Armenia	Cayman Islands	Eritrea
Aruba	Central Africa	Estonia
Australia	Chad	Ethiopia
Austria	Chile	Eurpoa Island
Azerbaijan	China	Falklands
Bahamas	Christmas Island	Faroe Islands
Bahrain	Cocos Islands	Fiji
Bangladesh	Columbia	Finland
Barbados	Comoros Congo	France
Belarus	Congo Republic	French Guiana
Belgium	Cook Islands	French Polynesia
Belize	Coral Sea Isles	Gabon
Benin	Costa Rica	Gambia
Bermuda	Cote d'Ivoire	Gaza Strip
Bhutan	Croatia	Georgia
Bolivia	Cuba	Germany
Bosnia	Cyprus	Ghana
Botswana	Czech Republic	Gibraltar

Glorioso Isles	Jordan	Mayotte
Greece	Juan de Nova	Mexico
Greenland	Kazakhstan	Micronesia
Grenada	Kenya	Moldova
Guadeluope	Kiribati	Monaco
Guam	Korea North	Mongolia
Guatemala	Kuwait	Monserrat
Guernsey	Kyrgyzstan	Morocco
Guinea	Laos	Mozambique
Guinea-Bissau	Latvia	Namibia
Guyana	Lebanon	Nauru
Haiti	Lesotho	Navassa Island
Honduras	Liberia	Nepal
Hong Kong	Libya	Netherlands
Hungary	Liechtenstein	New Caledonia
Iceland	Lithuania	New Zealand
India	Luxembourg	Nicaragua
Indonesia	Macau	Niger
Iran	Macedonia	Nigeria
Iraq	Malawi	Niue
Ireland	Malaysia	Norfolk Island
Isle of Man	Maldives	N Mariana Isles
Israel	Mali	Norway
Italy	Malta	Oman
Jamaica	Marshall Isles	Pakistan
Jan Mayen	Martinique	Palau
Japan	Mauritania	Pananma
Jersey	Mauritius	Papua N'Guinea

Countries of the world

Paracel Islands	Singapore	Tonga
Paraguay	Slovakia	Tromelin Island
Peru	Slovenia	Tunisia
Philippines	Solomon Islands	Turkey
Pitcairn Islands	Somalia	Turkmenistan
Poland	South Africa	Turks & Caicos
Portugal	South Georgia	Tuvalu
Puerto Rico	S Sandwich Isle	Uganda
Qatar	Spain	Ukraine
Reunion	Spratly Islands	United Arab Em
Romania	Sri Lanka	United Kingdom
Russia	Sudan	United States
Rwanda	Suriname	Uruguay
Saint Helena	Svalbard	Uzbekistan
StKitts & Nevis	Swaziland	Vanatu
Saint Lucia	Sweden	Vatican City
Saint Pierre	Switzerland	Venezuela
Saint Vincent	Syria	Vietnam
Samoa	Taiwan	Virgin Islands
San Marino	Tajikistan	Wake island
Sao Tome	Tanzania	Wales
Saudi Arabia	Thailand	Wallis & Futuna
Scotland	Timor-Leste	West Bank
Senegal	Togo	Western Sahara
Serbia	Tokelau	Yemen
Seychelles	Trinidad &	Zambia
Sierra Leone	Tobago	Zimbabwe

Use this list to highlight on pages 48-49 where in the world you have already been and to decide where you might like to go at some point in the future.

You may want to set yourself some goals in chapter 6 in order to make sure you get there one day!

Remember these are the Countries of the world, you may have been to various towns and cities in each of these countries or have travelled to the same country or place a number of times...

Everything you have written in this book is a way of recording where you are in your life and where you would like to be as you start secondary school. You will have had the opportunity to write down your goals, thoughts, ideas and dreams and to understand more about what's important to you as you go to secondary school.

Recording the things that you enjoy and the things that annoy you will help you identify things that you'd like to carry on doing and the things you'd like to change as you grow.

Now that you have filled it in, the book will become a keepsake for you to look back at in the future to help you to remember just how you felt and what you were hoping for at this time, helping you keep track and remember the story of your life in words, pictures, places, music and songs...

To find out more about something beginning with me..., visit our web-site:

www.sbwm.co

Other books in the series; something beginning with me...

- as I become a teenager

- at 18

- at 21

- as I start my first job

- as I move in to my first home

- as I get married